The Influencer's Path to Successful Publishing

Share Your Message, Cultivate Your Community, and Build Your Brand

April O'Leary and Heather Davis Desrocher
O'Leary Publishing

Ready to be an author?

Schedule Your 30-minute book
consultation today.

www.olearypublishing.com

O'LEARY
PUBLISHING
The Influencer's Press

TABLE OF CONTENTS

INTRODUCTION

Welcome to *The Influencer's Path to Successful Publishing* with the O'Leary Publishing Team. We're so glad you're here.

The publishing landscape has changed dramatically in recent years, opening many new doors to authors — both beginners and experienced. It's also exciting that non-writers now have the opportunity to be authors too. And perhaps the most notable change is the rise of high-quality, commercially successful self-published authors.

Independent authors are experiencing successes that would have been unreachable just ten years ago. At O'Leary Publishing we've had new authors hit #1 in their Amazon category in the first week their book launched with no prior experience, no website, and no social media following.

As a result, more and more people are choosing to publish independently rather than trying to navigate the traditional publishing industry. That said, there remains quite a bit of confusion about what self-publishing is, what options are open to authors, and how to publish successfully.

The term "self-publishing" is somewhat misleading. Just like making a film, publishing a book professionally requires more than one person. It's a team effort drawing on the diverse skills of many experts ranging from content editors, copy editors, graphic designers, photographers, interior designers, and public relations and distribution experts.

With roughly a million new books entering the market every year (and that's just in North America) it's more important than ever that authors ensure their books are as good as they can be, inside and out. This is why independent hybrid publishing has become so popular!

This guide explains how you can take your idea and turn it into a quality manuscript and publish a traditional quality book that will do well in the marketplace.

Whether you want to utilize our ghostwriting and interview process or write it yourself, we bring you from a rough draft to a professionally published book in less than 12 months.

I also share my personal (but not so pretty) path to publishing my first book as a life coach and leave you more confident and better prepared to publish a book you'll be proud to sign than I was at that time.

If you have any questions or would like a 30-minute book consultation please visit us at www.olearypublishing.com. We would love to listen to your idea and see if working with O'Leary Publishing could be the next step in your business or personal success story.

To your writing success,

April O'Leary and Heather Davis Desrocher
O'Leary Publishing
april@olearypublishing.com
heather@olearypublishing.com
www.olearypublishing.com

CHAPTER 1

APRIL'S (NOT SO PRETTY) PUBLISHING STORY

It was the first seven days I had to myself in seven years. Having been focused on mothering and building a life coaching business, the sight of my children driving away in an airport shuttle with my in-laws was exhilarating and scary. I knew what I had to do and yet I had never done it before.

Walking back inside a clean and quiet house I was feeling the labor pains. But these labor pains were not the same as the pains I experienced giving birth to my three daughters. These were the pains of having an idea and knowing, without a doubt, that I had to birth this idea into the world. I had been pregnant with it for a few years, ever since I discovered a practical way to manage my emotions in the midst of chaos and had been helping clients achieve the same despite overwhelming odds.

Yes, now was my time. I had to do it. But how?

With a yellow pad in hand, I wrote out the summary. I sketched out the table of contents. I made notes under each section with bullet points, to remind myself what stories I wanted to share in which chapters. And then...

I moved all the chairs away from the kitchen table except for one. I pushed it under the window facing the lake outside. And I sat. For seven days. I typed fast and furious. The contractions were strong, and the labor was intense. There was no time for rest. This baby had to be born, and there was no turning back.

At the end of the seven days, I remember vividly floating in my pool on a raft with the first draft of a manuscript in hand. It was like no feeling I can describe. I was proud of myself. But more than that, I was looking at this baby wondering how I was going to take care of it. What was next? I had no idea!

Just like leaving the hospital with an infant slumped over in a car seat, that butterflies in the stomach feeling returned. How was I supposed to DO this? Who would help me get this fledgling little print-out into a book format? How would I get it out into the world?

Like any smart person would do, I began researching publishing companies. I looked on my bookshelf at home and pulled off some of my favorite titles. Titles that represented, I thought, the same type of content that I was looking to publish. I took some notes from the Copyright pages of outfits I thought would be a good fit for me. And the good news is that I had experience in the PR/Media industry before this, so I had some good contacts of agents who had sent guests to the national radio show I used to guest produce.

I reached out to a few with little to no success. How many email subscribers did I have? How many Twitter followers? How was I going to sell the book? This confused me. Wasn't that THEIR job? I had the content. They pay me and sell it.

Not exactly...I would soon find out.

Being a visionary and sometimes too optimistic person, I signed up for a Writer's Workshop event put on within a few hours of my house by a large publisher who I was dreaming would someday be MY publisher. I had my manuscript printed out, and I envisioned running into the CEO and handing it off directly to him, and it would be a done deal.

I spent eight hours and hundreds of dollars just to find out that all a large publisher is interested in is "YOUR PLATFORM." How do you grab the attention of a major publisher? Build your community. Build your email list. Build your followers on Facebook and other social media platforms. THEN go pitch an idea to them via an agent or a book proposal (which they usually never accept unless you go through an agent).

After all, to a mainstream publisher, you are just a business investment. They have to know how they are going to sell your book and YOU are the way they are going to sell it. I left the one-day publishing event deflated but also empowered. If I have to sell my own book and build my own platform, what do I need a publisher for anyhow? Especially if they keep the rights to my book. How is that a good deal? I couldn't see the benefit.

The doors started to open in my mind, and I began a path to researching HOW I could make it happen. At this time I had no idea that there were other types of self-publishing companies out there that offered help for aspiring authors. So I spent many hours and a lot of money navigating my way through the often murky waters of hiring online help and working remotely with people I didn't know.

The bottom line is that I was able to do it. Now I will say that I am naturally extremely techy and understand the nuances of working online, so the project was completed successfully. To be honest, I don't know many people who have done the same. My first book *Ride the Wave: Journey to Peaceful Living* was a living, breathing book and I was thrilled.

Did I sell a lot of copies? I bet you're wondering. Not really.

At that time, I had a big heart and minimal marketing skills. I did what I knew to do. I spoke to a few local groups. I was interviewed on some podcasts and radio shows. And then I figured out that this book could be so much more. In fact, the book wasn't the end game at all!

I began creating a workbook and a journal. I developed an 8-week course which I taught online and locally. I spawned off two conference events from it as well. So this baby of a book brought so much more to my business than I ever could have imagined.

Since that time I have written three other books that reflect my growth and have created other business opportunities. Too many to list here. I've built friendships with people I would never have otherwise met. I've sifted through some personal challenges and written about them as I did in my most recent book *The Ultimate Love Affair: Awaken to God's Love in Just 40 Days.* Writing books, to me, is rewarding on so many levels. And the fact that doing so can help others far and wide is a tremendous blessing.

Imagine this small world story. I was sitting poolside during one of our author's book signing party and a lady I don't know approached me. We chat for a few minutes, and she says, "I enjoyed your blogs you wrote last year that you turned into your Love Affair book. Are you still writing them? I haven't seen any lately."

The truth is, I haven't been keeping up on my blog writing lately (for obvious reasons) and maybe I will get back to it. The conversation, which continued for probably twenty minutes, reminded me how important writing and sharing ideas are. It is a great way to reach others you may never meet in person. She told me she had forwarded every one of them to her friend in another state and they had discussed them. It was a time of healing for her after a season of much tragedy in her family.

Wow. I was humbled.

So the birth of O'Leary Publishing came from my own experience as a four-time author and the need I saw for a high-quality publishing service that could help the aspiring author avoid all the challenges I endured to get my first book out to market.

Our authors are treated like royalty. Because they are. Each one has a golden idea. Each one has experiences to share. Each one has a passion to help others. Each one is doing their best to live out their truth and share their message with as many others as possible.

And in the process, they too will find their book is not only about book sales. Although our authors have achieved some pretty serious credibility on Amazon reaching bestseller status in the first week of their launch, they know that is not the end game.

The end game is changing minds and hearts and lives. The end game is using their book to open other doors. The end game is building a community and a shared experience for others. The end game is so much more than a book.

Just like being pregnant with a baby and giving birth is not the end game to parenting. A parent understands that pouring their love and time and attention into another being and navigating challenges with them and celebrating successes with them and unwaveringly holding their hand through the unknown future of life together. That is parenting.

Authoring is no different. Authoring asks more of you. To be a bigger person. To lead as others cannot or will not lead. To not only surrender to your growth but to have the courage to put your ideas out in front of others who may not understand or accept them. Being an author is doing it anyway. Sure, anyone can write a story. But will they? Don't let your idea die inside of you. Take that giant leap of faith and birth that baby.

That is authoring.

We would love to work with you and hold your hand every step of the way. Take a peek now inside our publishing processes: From Inspiration to Manuscript, From Manuscript to Publication, Working With a Publishing Company and How to Get Started Today.

We have created this simple guide to help you effortlessly decide if Independent Hybrid

Publishing is right for you. It is what I wish I would have had access to before I struggled to publish my first book and what is now available to you. Let's get started.

CHAPTER 2

FROM INSPIRATION TO MANUSCRIPT

Completing a manuscript is one of the most exhilarating moments in a writer's life, and getting to that moment is also one of the greatest challenges. To help make sure you cross that finish line and have a working manuscript, here are our six top tips:

GHOSTWRITING. First, decide if you are ready to write a book yourself or whether you want to leave it to the experts. Being an author does not mean you need to sit down and type for hours at the computer or worse yet, look at a blank screen with writer's block wishing you knew how to put your idea on paper. It does mean that you have an idea to share and you want to have it published for personal or professional reasons.

The good news is that we, at O'Leary Publishing, are equipped to work with both writers and non-writers to help them develop and launch a book in a professional and timely manner that fits both their writing ability, availability, and accessibility. Many of our entrepreneurial clients find that their time is better spent working in their own business than it would be dedicating a large chunk of time to writing and we are ready to jump in and help them leverage their time in the best way possible.

WRITING IT YOURSELF. If you are a writer, we have a path for you too. Finishing a book is a challenge for anyone, but having a structure in place is a great way to improve your chances of reaching your goal. We help our clients stay focused. By working with a pre-determined rough outline and keeping the back cover summary top of mind, our authors can get their message is written without distraction. This method will help keep you going in the right direction as you craft your sentences, paragraphs, and chapters. Having an outline in place doesn't mean you can't make changes and improvements to the structure as you go along. Revise your outline as needed and know that having an idea of the direction you're headed is the best way to make sure you reach The End. Whether you've already completed your manuscript or you're just at the beginning phase of development we have a package that's just right for you.

CREATE A HABIT. Many writers begin their books in a blaze of inspiration, writing hundreds or even thousands of words in a single sitting. The problem, of course, is that we get tired. And distracted. And we just plain run out of time and energy. The focus to make a huge impact is to remember that your time spent writing is a top priority. In Steven Covey's book, *The 7 Habits of Highly Effective People*, he talks about working in Quadrant 2 as being the most valuable use of your time. This "Not Urgent but Important" is the most important for the long-term achievement of goals. Writing a book falls into that category. Look at the impact he's had with his book. Imagine if he hadn't written it!

	Urgent	Not Urgent
Important	**Quadrant 1** Crisis Pressing Problem Emergency	**Quadrant 2** **Book Writing** New Opportunities Growing Relationships Health and Recreation
Not Important	**Quadrant 3** Interruptions Emails, Calls, Texts Social Media Pressing Matters	**Quadrant 4** Trivial or Busy Work Time Wasters Pleasant Activities Some Calls and Emails

In writing, momentum is critical. The most powerful way to make quick and effective progress on your manuscript is to write a little every day. Even just 500 words each day would make a 35,000-word manuscript (the equivalent of 150 pages) in less than two months. Best of all, once you get into the habit of writing every day, it gets easier and easier to generate new ideas and improve your skills. Most importantly, keep in mind that you're not aiming for perfection — you're aiming for production. A terrible sentence is better than no sentence at all because you can't edit a blank page.

CREATE A TEAM. For all the joy of writing, the truth is that every writer struggles, every manuscript has its problems, and everyone can benefit from the help of others. A writing group and enlisting a team of "beta" readers for feedback is one of the best ways to get perspective on your work. A team can help you spot things you've missed and also help generate ideas to make your work stronger. Think about your friends or family as the first line of defense. They can become an excellent asset for feedback and constructive criticism as you write your manuscript. Your O'Leary Publishing team will also be by your side every step of the way to offer accountability and navigate roadblocks. They will keep you on track with our predetermined timeline so that your book doesn't remain a 'someday maybe' dream, it becomes a 'deadlined reality' that you can be proud of in the very near future.

PLAN FOR SUCCESS. Regardless of how you publish your book, the job of being a writer requires more than just writing. Every writer is the chief spokesperson for their book and, as such, is essential to the book's success. For better or worse, people want to hear from the author — how the book was written, where the idea came from, additional information, and so on. It's never too early to think about how you're going to market your book. Who is your audience? Why will your book be special to them? What can you do to help your book stand out against competing titles? Answering these questions as early as possible can go a long way toward supporting your book's ultimate success. Remember, every writer is also an "authorpreneur." We at O'Leary Publishing, also take pride in the process we provide to help our authors position their book in the marketplace for maximum exposure and reach. We don't drop you off the cliff with a book in hand, if you want us to, we can come alongside you in the post-publishing process to be sure your book reaches its intended audience.

KNOW WHEN TO STOP. Perhaps the most important thing to keep in mind is that your job as a writer is not to make the perfect manuscript. Your job is to make the best manuscript that you can on your own. Once you have your best manuscript, it's time to work with professionals who will help bring your writing to its full potential before publication. As Oscar Wilde told his editors, *"I'll leave you to tidy up the woulds and shoulds, wills and shalls, thats and whichs, etc."* That said, editors can do much, much more than correct spelling and grammar. We'll discuss editing further in upcoming sections of this guide. Every book that comes through O'Leary Publishing is given the same attention to detail and professionalism you would expect from a traditional publisher.

CHAPTER 3

FROM MANUSCRIPT TO PUBLICATION

Whether you utilize our book consulting services or not, congratulations! You are one of the very few who manage to complete a manuscript! Next comes deciding how you would like to publish it. Over the last decade, there has been enormous growth in the number of ways to get published, as well as the number of writers and companies competing for readers' time and attention. Although these publishing models can differ significantly, they can be broadly grouped into four categories: traditional, hybrid, vanity press, and self-publishing services.

TRADITIONAL PUBLISHING

This is the most well-known publishing model. In this scenario, a writer publishes his or her book via a publishing company, with the help of a literary agent. Publishing companies provide editing, design, and marketing services, and may provide a cash advance to an author who has a large platform and can sell many thousands of copies. Advances are usually "against royalties," which means that authors need to earn back their advance from book sales before actually earning additional royalty payments. Traditional publishing companies are primarily interested in a book's potential saleability. This makes it extremely difficult for new authors or those with an unusual subject matter, to breakthrough. The timeline for publishing traditionally from acquisition to release is generally 2 to 3 years.

HYBRID PUBLISHING

This model provides a top-quality publishing process that is accessible to an aspiring author. Hybrid publishing is popular amongst authors who desire a professional outcome that rivals the quality of a traditional publisher. The good news is that a hybrid publishing company can turn out a book in less than a year and potentially as little as 90 days and guides the author through every phase of the book publishing process for a package fee. The author decides how much or little involvement they want during the manuscript development, design, and post-publication phases. A hybrid publisher is highly invested in the outcome of the books they publish because they are adding their name to the cover and also share a % of the royalties. Therefore, the quality of the book, both inside and out, must be an A+.

VANITY PRESS PUBLISHING

A vanity press publisher is a publishing house that will lend its name to add credibility to your book and provide a templated design process. They create a perceived "I am a published author" feel for someone who does not want to spend the time or money on quality editing for their manuscript or cannot let go of their ideas and allow the input of professionals who aim to mold a manuscript into a masterpiece. Some vanity press companies provide a la carte options for aspiring authors but beware that their goal is to publish your book in whatever format you feel is best for you while offering very little professional input. Many have very low entry price points and will try to upsell you on all the bells and whistles. Because the quality of the book is compromised by allowing the customer to pick and choose what is important to them, the books often don't sell as well or appear competitive due to the lack of guidance.

SELF-PUBLISHING SERVICES

This model is represented by companies like KDP, IngramSpark, Lulu, and others but can also include independent printers. In this model, authors have 100% control and responsibility to produce every aspect of their book themselves. They upload their final files for publication directly inside these platforms. Self-publishing websites provide no editing, book design, marketing, or promotional support, which also makes them the quickest, cheapest way to publish and allows authors to retain the highest percentage of a book's selling price. However, because self-published books are not professionally produced or supported, quality and sales volumes tend to be very low.

Unlike many "self-publishing" companies, O'Leary Publishing authors work with a dedicated project manager who guides and oversees all stages of their book's production. Each book receives a customized book publishing timeline, consulting throughout the manuscript writing process, an editor's manuscript evaluation, and full access to a developmental editor, a line editor, and a proofreader. They also receive custom book interior layout, and custom cover design, as opposed to the automated, template approach adopted by many other firms.

Once your book nears completion, you'll gain access to a book marketing strategy session to help you create a plan to maximize your book's sales success. We can also coordinate post-publishing services such as: organizing a successful book launch both online and offline, developing a PR/Media packet, creating an online book sales funnel with upsell strategies woven in to generate additional income, running Facebook ad campaigns, and driving traffic and attention to your book yielding some of our authors #1 Best Seller status on Amazon the first week of their book launch.

Our project cycles last from 90 days to 12 months depending on the number and scope of services you require. Unlike many other publishing services providers, we stay partnered with you after your book is published offering promotional support and a royalty program that will maximize your chances of earning a solid return on your investment.

The O'Leary Publishing Team is located in the United States in Naples, Florida, and we work with clients around the country as we are available via Zoom and utilize a dedicated file sharing system between our team and our authors.

CHAPTER 4

WORKING WITH A PUBLISHING COMPANY

Choosing a publishing partner is a major decision for any author. At O'Leary Publishing, we understand the importance of each book. We do our utmost to return the trust authors place in us by delivering the highest-quality services available anywhere.

The path to the successful publishing of your book has five distinct steps:

STEP 1: READ *THE INFLUENCER'S PATH TO SUCCESSFUL PUBLISHING*

Guess what? You are already completing Step 1 right now! It is important to understand the basic process of publishing, what is involved to develop your idea into a manuscript format, and the types of publishing options that are available to aspiring authors today. This will help you decide if moving forward to Step 2 with O'Leary Publishing makes sense for you.

STEP 2: SCHEDULE A 30-MINUTE BOOK CONSULT

The next step on your publishing journey is to chat with someone on our team. We will answer any questions you may have and ask you some strategic questions about your book so that we can recommend the best publishing experience for you.

Among the questions we will ask are:

What is your book about?

Different genres have different conventions regarding design, editing, and promotion. Knowing what kind of book you plan to write will help us explain the options open to you and help you make the best decisions for your book. We will also advise you on researching the market for similar, possibly competing, books. We'll help you strategically position your book to sell.

Why is this book important to you?

Knowing why you want to write your book will help us recommend the best path for you. We want to know whether your goal is to share your expertise more widely, build a growing brand or leave a legacy for your family. Any of these are great reasons to write a book.

What's your budget and time frame to launch?

Publishing a book is a labor of love, but it is also an investment. You'll want to make sure your book has the resources it needs to succeed in the marketplace. We also understand that some topics are extremely time-sensitive and need to be rushed to market. We will help you determine the timeline that is right for you and your book.

Is your manuscript done?

Our goal is to help you plan for success. If you have made it through Steps 1 and 2 and you're ready to move forward, we offer two options for aspiring authors after their 30-minute consultation. Based on the answer to the previous questions, we will recommend either Step 3a or 3b. Don't worry. We will guide you every step of the way!

To schedule your 30-minute book consultation, please visit www.olearypublishing.com/contact-us.

STEP 3A: SCHEDULE A BOOK MAPPING SESSION

Having a focused topic and layout for your book is essential for any writer, especially if we are ghostwriting your book for you. This is the next step for you if you do not have a manuscript written. You do not need to know how to organize your idea or lay it out in a logical table of contents. We will help you with that. This step will help you further your commitment and clarity to write your book. During this two-hour mind-mapping session, we will get into the trenches with you and help you flesh out your book idea.

Our team will ask strategic questions and help you clarify why you want to write your book, who it is going to help, and what you plan to do with it when it is done. You'll walk away from this session with the back cover copy of your book written, a handful of possible title and subtitle ideas, the table of contents mapped out, and the specific word-count-per-chapter defined. Your book will be timelined based on the proposed length and the pacing for publishing will be planned. We ensure that all of the details feel right for your goals.

Once the book mapping is complete, you'll have a path to publication that is clear and concise. You won't have to stare at a blank computer screen, wondering what you're going to write. You'll have a road map to get there. The book map is, of course, yours to keep; we do not retain the rights to any of the ideas we generate from the session nor does it require you to publish with us, or at all. We simply hope that you will see the vision for your book, and gain the confidence you need so that you can commit to writing it.

STEP 3B: SCHEDULE A MANUSCRIPT REVIEW

This step is for you if you have already written your manuscript. A manuscript review will help you gain valuable insight about your prospective book. Your book will be read by our editorial team, and you will receive a report that details the strengths and weaknesses of your manuscript. You'll be given concrete ideas to improve your book and an overview of other titles that are competing, successfully, in your genre and category. Your review includes a 30-minute Zoom meeting to discuss the report and the steps forward to the successful publication of your book.

Since we customize the publishing packages of our aspiring authors based on the estimated amount of work involved with a project, this is a critical step for us. It is during this time that we will also determine if your book fits our mission to *raise global consciousness* and if we are the best publishing company for you. We do not publish all manuscripts we review; however, we do enjoy offering feedback to help you create a book that matters to you.

STEP 4: WE CREATE A BOOK PUBLISHING PROPOSAL

After completing Steps 3a and 3b, we will know if you are a good fit for publication with O'Leary Publishing. If you are not, we will be happy to refer you to one of our publishing colleagues who may be a better fit for your book. We are very specific with the book genres and types of authors we publish.

If we decide that you and your project are compatible with our publishing company, we will email you a detailed proposal for your book's publication. The fees paid in Step 3 are deducted from your package price if you sign a contract with us within 60 days of your manuscript review.

The book publishing proposal includes:

- ✓ Dedicated project manager
- ✓ Detailed timeline for publication
- ✓ Professional proofreading for grammar, punctuation, and English nuances
- ✓ Custom paperback cover design with three revisions
- ✓ Custom ebook cover design; formatting based on the final cover
- ✓ Custom interior book design; includes up to 10 images and two revisions
- ✓ Development of ebook file formats (.mobi and .epub)
- ✓ International Standard Book Numbers (ISBN) for print and ebook (and one reserved for audiobook if needed)

- ✔ Registration with the US Copyright Office
- ✔ Electronic book proof
- ✔ Paperback publication distributed online
- ✔ Ebook distribution – Kindle, Apple iTunes, Google Play, B&N Nook
- ✔ Author copies available at wholesale pricing
- ✔ Book one-sheet for media interviews

All editorial services are billed monthly. The amount of editorial support necessary for your book is based on the length of your manuscript, your writing skill, and is only billed based on the number of hours of assistance needed. The various types of editing such as developmental editing and line editing are outlined in your book proposal. To get started, we require a 25 percent deposit on your publishing package; the remaining fees will be billed monthly throughout your project. A typical project lasts between six and nine months.

STEP 5: YOU RECEIVE A BOOK CONTRACT

If all the stars have aligned and you receive a book contract based on the book proposal you reviewed (as outlined in Step 4), we congratulate you. Working with a publishing partner, like O'Leary Publishing, is the final step to becoming a published author. While there are many independent book publishing companies to choose from, we believe that the quality of our authors, the beauty of the books we publish, and the attention you will receive throughout the process are second to none.

We aim to make your book publishing experience one you will enjoy. We are building a community of authors who support one another and are changing the world together. When you choose to publish with O'Leary Publishing, you are not just getting a book in hand, you are gaining a publishing family.

Once the book contract is signed and the deposit is received, we will schedule your onboarding call. We (April and Heather) are excited to welcome you aboard and will share the technical details of your project's management. We will generate a project timeline, working toward your desired publication date.

In addition to publishing your book, we offer some bells and whistles to help your book sail into the marketplace successfully. These are things you will want to consider as you are launching your book into the world.

POST-PUBLICATION SERVICES

Here at O'Leary Publishing, we believe that we must help you maximize your efforts to get your book in the hands of as many readers as possible. While you might come to us with a large email subscriber list, or a growing podcast, or have some media relations experience, it is helpful to have a plan when you launch your book using all available resources.

During the book publishing and design process, we talk about strategic placement of marketing – either in the front matter (the first few pages) of your book or somewhere on the cover. Your book is the first step on the reader's journey with you. What comes next? This needs to be very clear to the reader.

We love to help you think through the logical next steps any reader might take. Would they download Chapter 1 free from your website, then purchase your book, and then schedule a consultation with you? Is it more logical that they would purchase your book first, then download resources that support the book, and then come to a workshop you're hosting? Are you planning to sell additional merchandise? These are all important questions to ask as you plan the strategy for your book.

Our post-production services range from building out your website – complete with an email marketing plan and a shopping cart, so you can sell signed copies – to hosting a live speaker event for you. Or, we can help launch you with a Zoom party online. We also have a strategy to help you utilize a Facebook group to connect your audience to your forthcoming book – a strategy that has successfully helped 50 percent of our authors achieve #1 New Release status on Amazon in their designated category.

The post-publication services we offer will be discussed during the process of book production. We will help you assess your goals and create a plan to maximize your time and leverage your talents. In the meantime, we will fill in the gaps where we can add value to your project.

We always keep future revenues and business opportunities for the author in mind and will help you find ways to garner more attention and sell – not only more books but other products or services, with your book as the door opener to so much more. Speaking events. Selling branded items online. Building a membership community. We can do any combination that fits your business and/or personal goals.

Each author's journey is as unique as each author. While there is no prescribed path to ultimate success, the book will certainly bring you rewards that you never could have expected.

CHAPTER 5

HOW TO GET STARTED TODAY

Remember what Steven Covey says, "*The most important things you'll do in life are not urgent but they are important.*" Writing a book is one of those very things.

Now imagine showing up for a business lunch and bringing your book with you as a gift for a prospective new client. Imagine searching your name on Amazon, and your book comes up with an orange "Best Seller" label next to the front cover. Imagine strangers emailing you asking for a meeting or telling you how much you changed their lives. This is not only possible. It's likely.

As a trained life coach this is one thing I would often ask my clients. Why wait? Often the things we can easily put off until tomorrow, or next week or next year are the things that, if we did them now, would have the most impact on our business and life.

Think about it. The twenty pounds someone carries around can sit on their waist, and they can try to hide it indefinitely until it becomes fifty pounds or a hundred pounds extra. And then they are forced to address the problem because it is no longer an annoyance it's a crisis.

Why not take action and eliminate the twenty pounds while it's easy and then enjoy the benefits of looking better and having more energy without waiting until you're forced to fix it?

Likewise, in business, there are sometimes lingering problems with systems and processes that need addressing for maximum functionality. But more of a distraction is that often business is cranking along as usual and the little extra time and money that could be spent on separating yourself from a crowded marketplace are ignored. Why bother? Why put forth the extra effort? Things are okay now.

But what if they could be great. What if a book could help you leverage your time to reach more people and spread your message and attract more business because you are now a leader in your field. What if the ideas that swirl around in your head and wake you up at night are not just for you...what if they are divinely given for you to share with the world.

What if…

Don't wonder. Today is the time to take action. Visit www.olearypublishing.com to book your 30-minute book consultation today.

We look forward to hearing from you.

O'LEARY
PUBLISHING
The Influencer's Press

O'Leary Publishing provides independent hybrid book publishing services for brands, professionals, and entrepreneurs. We bring you from idea to print effortlessly through a proven system that is especially effective for non-writers and those who would prefer to leave the writing to an expert. For more about our services visit www. olearypublishing.com.